How to Use Biblical Love
in Human Relationships

How to Use Biblical Love in Human Relationships:

How to Discipline the Way Jesus Was Disciplined

by

Doris Sharbaugh

The Whitston Publishing Company
Troy, New York
1990

Library of Congress Catalog Card Number 89-51927

ISBN 0-87875-393-1

Printed in the United States of America

Dedicated to my grandchildren,
Jennifer, Erika, Dale, Timothy,
Durell Dean Jr. and Sarah

Contents

Acknowledgements

I wish to express my deep appreciation for the encouragement, support and professional knowledge so freely given in the preparation of the manuscript. If Pastor David Giles had not shared some of his knowledge of the Bible scriptures with me, I would not have written the manuscript. Professor of Theology, Neva Miller, wrote the chapter **Understanding Biblical Love** and critically reviewed the first draft of the manuscript. Professors of psychology, I. M. Abou-Gohrra and Paul Centi, reviewed the first draft of the manuscript and provided helpful suggestions and encouragement. Numerous ministers reviewed the manuscript and offered suggestions and encouragement. Doris Hastings, instructor of a creative writing class, reviewed the final draft of the manuscript. Dr. Wm. Kelley, psychologist and director of a Christian counseling service, reviewed the final draft of the manuscript. Loretta Parks helped in many ways. My husband, Amandus, supported my education in human action and reaction and my efforts to teach and use the principles of Biblical love. Professor of Psychology, K. Koppe, spent personal time, beyond regular class hours, to answer my questions during my study of human action and reaction.

For permission to quote material copyrighted by the following, or in some sense belonging to them, I wish to express my grateful appreciation:

Your Child's Self-Esteem, by Dorothy Corkille Briggs
(Copyright 1975 by Dorothy Corkille Briggs, published byDoubleday & Co., Inc., a division of Bantam, Doubleday, Dell Publishing Group, Inc., New York, NY.)

Bringing Out the Best in Your Baby, by Art Ulene, M.D. and Steven Shelov, M.D.
(Copyright 1986 by Art Ulene and Steve Shelov, published by Macmillan Publishing Co., New York, NY.)

Coping with Teenage Depression, by Kathleen McCoy
(Copyright 1982 by Kathleen McCoy, published by NAL [New American Library], a division of Penguin Books USA, Inc., New York, NY.)

Controlling Stress & Tension, by Dr. Daniel A. Girdano and Dr. George Everly
(Copyright 1986 by Dr. Daniel A. Girdano and Dr. George Everly, published by Prentice-Hall, Inc., Englewood Cliffs, NJ.)

Dr. Spock's Baby and Child Care, 40th anniversary edition, by Benjamin Spock, M.D. and Michael B. Rothenberg, M.D.
(Copyright 1985 by Benjamin Spock and Michael B. Rothenberg, published by Pocket Books, Simon & Schuster Inc., New York, NY.)

Parent Effectiveness Training, by Thomas Gordon
(Copyright 1976 by Thomas Gordon, published by

Foreword

The goal of this book is to teach how to use Biblical love (as described in 1 Corinthians 13:4-11) and how to discipline in the loving way Jesus was disciplined as a means of preventing and dealing with human disharmony, physical fighting, divorce, child abuse, spouse abuse, parent abuse, crime, terrorism, violence, and war.

When we understand human action and reaction, we agree with the Bible passage, "When love prevails, the imperfect disappears." I Corinthians 13:4-11, gives the elements of love. However, it does not explain the most effective way known to man to be unselfish, kind, non-blaming, patient, truthful and protective. Loving words and actions promote the spirit of love. Unloving words and actions negatively affect the spirit of love.

In an effort to encourage love and peace in relationships we must know how to resolve conflicts, rectify wrongdoing, and act and speak in a loving manner.

This book explains common misinterpretations of Bible passages which promote disharmony and the emotional as well as the physical destruction of man. It gives help in understanding human action and reaction, stressing children's needs and their related behavior.

This book analyzes the kind and non-blaming manner in which Jesus was disciplined as it is revealed in Luke 2:41-52. It also explains how to teach right from wrong and correct unacceptable behavior in the same kind and non-blaming manner. This loving method of correcting unacceptable behavior and teaching right from wrong can be used in adult relationships as well as disciplining children.

Personal experiences illustrate the Biblical theory, "When love prevails, the imperfect disappears."

This composition is not intended to be a complete text of human action and reaction or a complete child-raising guide. A number of books which support kind, unselfish and non-blaming parental actions are listed at the end of the book.

Each chapter is written so that it will be valuable as a separate study hoping the book could be used piece-meal by busy clergymen, parents, teachers or others, as well as a complete study.

Methods of Resolving Conflicts and
Teaching Right from Wrong

Society uses two main methods to resolve conflicts, to correct wrongdoing, and to teach right from wrong. One method is the use of man's God-given ability to reason in a kind and unselfish manner. Reasoning in a loving mode includes kind verbal communication, knowing how to resolve conflicts with compromises, and attacking a problem in a kind and non-blaming manner rather than attacking the offender. Jesus was disciplined with this method. As an adult, Jesus used reasoning and oral communication to teach and to resolve conflicts. (The chapter **Love is Kind** analyzes the way Jesus was disciplined, and describes how to correct wrongdoing and teach right from wrong using this loving approach, which can be used in all relationships.)

The other method of resolving conflicts is the use of unkind actions of power, such as unkind threats, unkind force, hitting and killing. The most powerful party wins. This method of dealing with others is the attitude used in physical fights, child abuse, spouse abuse, crime, terrorism, violence and war.

Children learn to relate to others from their parents' example in dealing with them. If a child has learned to hit others from his parents' example of hitting him, then it is necessary to *reteach* the child. He must learn that hitting is not loving behavior; otherwise, he may become an adult who will use unkind power as a means of solving problems.

Unkind power as a means of dealing with others existed before Christ, but the life of Jesus gives us insights into a better method of disciplining children, correcting wrongdoing, and resolving conflicts. Mary and Joseph set the example of disciplining in a verbal, non-blaming and non-power manner. Jesus set the example of relating to others in a kind verbal mode. Yet, through the ages, man has not been fully convinced of the advantages of disciplining children and relating to others in a kind, non-power manner. This is especially true of those who *have not been taught* to interpret the word "rod" (used in the text, "He who spares the rod") as "He who spares kind guidance and correction," rather than, "He who spares hitting the child." (The interpretations of the word "rod" as used in the Bible are explained in the chapter, **A Great Error in Bible Interpretation**, a chapter which also explains the undesirable results of using the "rod" in an unkind manner.)

If both native and newly-settled Americans had known, as children, how to resolve conflicts verbally, in a kind, compromising manner, there undoubtedly would not have been the need for guns or bows and arrows (unkind power) to resolve disputes over land possessions. We can even speculate that, if both the United States and the Soviet leaders had been disciplined as children with verbal, kind reasoning as an example to follow, rather than witnessing unkind power, the need for power to satisfy their emotional need to control, and the need to be able to resolve conflict with unkind power would not have resulted in the present arms race. Hopefully, man will use his God-given ability to reason in a loving manner to eradicate this problem.

Child abuse would not exist if the abusers had learned to deal with children in a *kind* manner. Spouse and parent abuse would not exist if the abusers had not learned abusiveness from their parents' example of abusing them. The majority of youth and adults who commit crimes were emotionally and physically abused children.

If the people who engage in violence had been disciplined with kind reasoning rather than unkind power when they were children, they would have learned, from their parents' example, how to resolve conflict in a kind rather than unkind manner.

Our school systems teach language as a means of human communication, but many do not teach how to communicate and resolve conflicts in a kind and compromising manner. Would it not be reasonable to spend tax dollars to educate children and adults from this point of view rather than to spend tax dollars for jails, weapons, and war?

Our religious leaders should be responsible for emphasizing the importance of Biblical love and the advantages of disciplining in the loving manner in which Jesus was disciplined.

Understanding Biblical Love

The greatest commandments which God gave are mentioned in Matthew 22:37 (NIV), "Jesus replied: 'Love the Lord your God with all your heart and with all your soul and with all your mind. . . . And the second is like it: Love your neighbor as yourself.'" John 15:12 (NIV) states that Jesus said, "My command is this: Love each other as I love you." The ten commandments are based mostly on love for God and love for man.

The Greek language has four main terms used for love: storge-"affection": philia-"friendship": eros-"passion": agape-"love." Two of these are used in the Greek New Testament, agape "love" and philia "friendship." The concept of storge is present in the Bible as it refers to family relationships, but the word itself does not occur. Eros is not used in the Bible: however, that does not mean it does not have its proper place in divinely created human sexuality. The Greek word "agape" is the word used for love in 1 Corinthians 13 and mostly elsewhere in the New Testament. It is used especially to refer to an attitude resulting from a conscious choice of the will. It is expressed in devotion and loyalty, and is behind agreements and covenants that prove firm and inviolable. It is used of both divine and human love.

Jesus gave the word "agape" a new and intensified meaning" "My command is this: Love each other as I love you." He made agape the fulfillment of all commands and the characteristic of all righteousness. Agape, since it is based in the will, can be commanded. "Thou shalt love . . . " said Jesus. This love is based on evaluation, potential application, choice and decision. Since love is a matter of will and action, Jesus demanded decision toward God and readiness for action in obedience to God in an unconditional manner that startled his hearers. Jesus called for a life wholly grounded in love, which could even overcome enemies, and never failed in achieving what it set out to do. Agape love is a power which brings true freedom separation from evil, high calling, and a sure expectation for the future. Thus, God's love is based on the high value He places upon us and the choice He has made of us. When we accept His love within us as the source of our own power to love, and the love that God shows for us becomes the inspiration and example for our own love, then 1 Corinthians becomes a possibility that can be lived out in our own lives.

Biblical Love is the basis for **Emotional Maturity**, which is the foundation for love and peace between friends and nations, for relationships between husband and wife, parent and child and employee and employer.

Biblical Love in Action

In 1 Corinthians 13:4-11, love is defined as patience, kindness, unselfishness and lack of jealousy, rudeness or irritability. Love does not boast, is not proud, does not judge, is slow to anger. Love does not delight in evil, but rejoices in the truth. It always protects, always trusts, always hopes, always perserveres. Love never fails. When love prevails, the imperfect (wrong) disappears. When love prevails, there is no need for unkind actions and punishment to resolve conflict, correct error, or teach right from wrong.

God is the supreme psychologist. He knows the workings of the human mind, the nature of human feelings, as well as human action and reaction. He created man and gave man the knowledge of Biblical love as a guideline for the good of all people, including children. Luke 2:41-52 reveals that Mary and Joseph disciplined Jesus in a kind, verbal and non-blaming manner. He lived an adult life of Biblical love. The Bible explains that peace will not prevail until Jesus returns to the earth.

Man must follow the examples of Mary, Joseph and Jesus in an effort to promote love and peace on earth. To use Biblical love as a means of promoting love and peace, it is necessary to teach man how to resolve conflicts and how to act and speak in a loving manner, especially in parent-child relationships.

The Bible instructs parents to bring up their children in the way they should go. Children learn how to relate to others in a kind way from their parents' kind example in dealing with them. The child's knowledge of how best to relate to others in a loving manner will be carried into adult behavior.

Children have the same emotional feelings as adults. To distinguish between *kind* words, actions and correction, and *unkind* words, actions and correction, use God's law: (Luke 6:31 NIV and Matthew 7:12 NIV) "Do to others as you would have them do to you."

Ask yourself, "If I were a child and my action needed to be corrected, would I feel angry, resentful, hostile, defiant, rebellious, unloved and rejected if spoken to or corrected in an unkind way? Or would I feel loved, and would I be cooperative if spoken to or taught in a loving, kind and unblaming manner?"

It is written in Ephesians 6:4 (NIV), "Fathers [authority], do not exasperate your children [provoke them to anger]; instead, bring them up in the training and instruction of the Lord [in a loving manner as described in 1 Corinthians 13:4-11]."

Adults and children resent dominating, unkind, selfish, blaming, unreasonable, impatient, forcing, nagging or rude authority over them. Resentment causes anger. Anger, in turn, can cause defiance, negativism, hostility, aggression, hatred, a need to get even, or a need for yet another act which will bring about more disapproval. Colossians 3:21 (NIV) instructs fathers, saying, "Fathers, do not embitter your children or they will become discouraged."

Children want kind discipline and want to please

adults. Parents who bring up their children in the training and instruction of the Lord (in the loving manner in which Jesus was disciplined) *will not provoke* them to anger or discourage them.

It is also necessary for parents to understand their children's growing stages, as well as their emotional and physical needs in order to avoid provoking them to anger or discouraging them. The book *Bringing Out the Best in Your Baby* by Art Ulene, M.D. and Steven Shelov, M.D. gives a good understanding of children's growing stages from birth to age four.

One example of the need to get even with unkind authority was when I, as a five-year-old child, deliberately sat in a mud puddle to "get even" with an impatient babysitter who had pulled my ear as a means of forcing me to hurriedly take a bath and put on clean clothes. Sixty years later, I visited with this babysitter. She reminded me of this childhood incident, but she did not associate her unkind forcing with my "need" to sit in the mud puddle! I did not have the heart to explain that it had been a direct reaction to her unkindness.

Another example involves a mother who continually forced her child into blind obedience but was not aware that her child had found a way to get even with her. The child knew that cooperating in his toilet training was the one thing his mother could not force him to do in spite of her begging, pleading, threatening or praising. His face beamed with a smile of delight when his mother could not succeed in forcing him. When he went to kindergarten with diapers on and realized that the other children no longer wore them he was embarrassed and finally cooperated in his toilet training. Later he found other means of getting even with his forcing parent.

I listened to the expressed feelings of a minister's daughter who had robbed stores as a means of retaliation for her father's overly strict, forceful and unkind discipline. He forced her to leave their home. I phoned the father hoping that they could resolve the problem. The father refused to have anything to do with his daughter. He blamed her for her unacceptable actions rather than recognizing the fact that his unloving actions had caused the problem. In retaliation for her father's rejection, the daughter married a person of whom he highly disapproved. She continued to rob stores until she was put in jail for her thievery. She was delighted that the newspapers published her actions. She knew this would further humiliate her father—a minister's daughter in jail for stealing!

Children, Obey Your Parents in the Lord

The bible gives instruction to children in Ephesians 6:1-3 (NIV) as follows: "Children, obey your parents *in the Lord*, for this is right. Honor your father and mother—which is the first commandment with a promise—that it may go well with you and that you may enjoy long life on the earth."

An error in Bible interpretations is the understanding of the phrase, "Children, obey your parents," which omits the phrase "*in the Lord.*" This would infer that children are to obey parents indiscriminately. The Bible clearly states that children are to *obey parents in the Lord's way.* This means that children are not expected to obey parental prejudices, unkindness, selfishness, (such as using the child for sexual pleasure) or any other actions that are wrong for the child. The phrase "in the Lord," also means that parents are to love their children and treat them in a loving manner, which is described in 1 Corinthians 13.

The greatest error in my lifetime was obeying my father indiscriminately. My younger eight-year old brother died as the result of our obedience to our father's unloving actions. Hearing a child cry, complain, ask questions or talk in his presence annoyed our father. He would whip us with a razor strap when we did anything to annoy him. My young brother developed appendicitis.

He cried in silence for a week. Although in pain, he was afraid to cry out or complain because he knew that our father would punish him. At times, I sat by his bedside watching him cry in silence, but I, too, was afraid to say anything to my father. It was not until my brother's last dying hours that my father realized he needed medical help. My father called the physician. The doctor immediately took my brother to the hospital. He operated, only to find that it was too late to save his life. My father blamed the doctor for my brother's death, not realizing it was his non-loving actions that were responsible. If our father had allowed us to express feelings, he would have known my brother was extremely ill, and would have called the physician in time to save his life. My brother and I *were obedient to our father's selfish needs, which resulted in my brother's death rather than the Biblical promise of a long life on this earth.*

Surely, it is not God's intention for children to be influenced by (obey) their parent's prejudices. One day, at the age of fifteen, as usual I went to my parents' home after school. My six foot, two-hundred and fifty pound strong father, who was a farmer, met me at the door with a horse-harness strap. Not a word was spoken. He grabbed me and held me by the arm with one hand and, in raging anger, whipped me with the other hand for about fifteen minutes. I screamed from pain during the whipping and cried after my painful experience. My father beat me again for crying. After the beating, I was so physically sore, I could barely move. I went to school the next day as a means of getting away from him. I asked my gym teacher if I could be excused from participating in the activities. She asked, "Why?" I couldn't tell her why because I knew if any news had gotten back to my father that I had complained, I would have been beaten again. My gym teacher suspected my problem. She took my sweater off and observed that I had huge welts all over my back. I never knew why my father whipped me, nor did I have the courage to ask him. Finally, when I was approximately sixty-five years old, I asked my mother why my father had done this to me. My mother explained that she thought it was because I had spoken to a classmate whose father was Republican. My father was a staunch Democrat. H e was a narrow-minded and opinionated person who would not tolerate any views that differed from his. He had one sister who was Republican. She lived only three-quarters of a mile from our house. My father seldom spoke to her and influenced me to avoid her.

Children who have been taught to obey authority indiscriminately are inclined to obey the pressures of peers as well as adults. In other words, they have not been allowed to defend or stand up for themselves even when it is for their good. The result is that they give in to peer pressures to indulge in sex, drugs, alcohol, cults, ride in an automobile or motorcycle with a person who is known to be a dangerous speeder, or follow other harmful suggestions. I made many mistakes during my youth and early adult years because I felt I had to obey others indiscriminately, just as I was forced to obey my father.

The passage, Ephesians 6:2, instructs children to "Honor your father and your mother." To be honored, one has to be honorable.

The abusing of parents has become a concern of today's society. It has been repeatedly observed that older children who abuse their parents were once children who were abused by their parents. In other words, the child learned his abusiveness from his parents' example in dealing with them.

I was emotionally and physically abused as the result of the religious belief "spare the rod, spoil the child" ("rod" meaning to inflict pain). My parents did not realize that God gave young children a sense of curiosity as a means of wanting to learn about their new environment. Rather than "child-proofing" my environment (which is explained in the chapter, **Love Protects**) and allowing me to explore and examine my new environment, I was spanked and whipped with a razor strap until my curiosity was curbed and I was driven into a state of depression. I lived in constant fear and anxiety, not knowing when the next blow of unkindness would come. This tension made me a nervous (hyper) child with the inability to sleep well. I also had frequent headaches, nausea, dizziness and stomach problems which resulted from the nervous tension. I knew my father would be annoyed if I complained or cried; therefore, I had to be silent.

In an effort to avoid my parents' unkind actions— especially those of my father—I spent as much time as possible alone in my room. Sometimes I would wander off aimlessly. Often, my parents could not find me, but then immediately spanked me when they had me in their reach. At that time I had no idea why I was spanked. I had no television, radio or books to use as a means to escape the thought of my unpleasant childhood; therefore, I would resort to day dreaming and cuddling my stuffed teddy bear to create the feeling of being loved. I found the same satisfaction in cuddling small animals.

As the result of having my curiosity curbed and falling into mental depression, I had little incentive for accomplishment, including schoolwork. However, going to school did give me the opportunity to get away from my father. He was a farmer and spent most of his time at home. My teachers would reprimand me for being "spaced out" (day dreaming) rather than listening to them and doing my school work. The only way I knew how to relate to other children was in the unkind way my father related to me; therefore, I had very few friends.

Fortunately, during my high school years, I became acquainted with a boy my age. He accepted me in spite of my emotional immaturity. I observed the loving relationship he had with his parents and his emotional maturity. Also, I noticed that he was disciplined with kind verbal reasoning and praised for anything he attempted to do.

My boyfriend and I were married after we graduated from college. After the birth of our first son, I studied human action and reaction as a means to overcome some of my emotional immaturity. Also, I learned how to discipline children with kind reasoning. Then our second son was born.

A problem arose. My husband and I had taken our two young sons to visit my parents, who lived on a farm. We asked my father if our oldest son could take a brief ride on one of his horses. He agreed that he could. We helped our son to mount the horse on his bare back without a riding harness, which was the way I rode horses during my childhood. We instructed our child to hold the horse's mane so he could not fall off, which he did. I had planned to gently lead the horse while our son took his ride. Instead, my father struck the horse quite hard to get action. The horse lunged and threw our son head first onto a rough, graveled driveway. Our son lay motionless. I was frightened that he may have broken his neck. My father laughed with great delight and said, "That will teach him to hang on!" Fortunately, our son's neck was not broken, but he was severely bruised and scraped from the rough stones. At that point, I felt that I did not want to take our children to visit my father again. For the first time in my life, I stood up to my father's abusiveness. I told him that if he ever did anything like that again, or if he struck our children in any way, I would never let them visit him again. To my amazement and relief, he accepted and conformed to my ultimatum. With the exception of this incident, our children never knew my father to be the abusive person he had been with me.

My experience with my father is an example of how children can improve family relationships by teaching unkind parents to be more loving. This can truly promote honor for the parent.

Love Is Kind, Love Does Not Blame

The parents of Jesus practiced kindness to discipline their son. Luke 2:41-52 (NIV) reveals that they attacked the problem rather than their son.

> Every year His parents went to Jerusalem for the Feast of the Passover. When He was twelve years old, they went up to the Feast, according to the custom. After the Feast was over, while His parents were returning home, the boy Jesus stayed behind in Jerusalem but they were unaware of it. Thinking He was in their company, they traveled on for a day. Then they began looking for Him among their relatives and friends. When they did not find Him, they found Him in the temple courts, sitting among the teachers, listening to them and asking them questions. Everyone who heard Him was amazed at His understanding and His answers. When His parents saw Him, they were astonished. His mother said to Him, "Son, why have you treated us like this? Your father and I have been anxiously searching for you.

Mary's words tell us that she and Joseph, as parents, attacked the problem, not their child. To attack the problem, His mother obviously tried to understand His action when she asked, "Why have you treated us like this?" So that Jesus would understand their problem, Mary explained *how* she and Joseph felt (anxious) and *what* caused them to feel as they did (the search for their son). Observe that Mary and Joseph did not blame, punish, or reprimand Jesus for His unacceptable behavior. Nor did they use an unkind or unexplained command to discipline Him, such as, "Don't do that again."

> "Why were you searching for me?" he asked. "Didn't you know I had to be in my Father's house?" But they did not understand what He was saying to them. Then He went down to Nazareth with them and was obedient to them. But His mother treasured all these things in her heart. And Jesus grew in wisdom and stature, and in favor with God and man.

Observe that Jesus was obedient and did not repeat the previous action because He obviously understood the problem He had created for His parents.

God selected Mary and Joseph to be the parents of Jesus. We may assume that God knew they would provide the childhood background and discipline that would enable Jesus to become the loving and wise person He was as an adult.

To practice the disciplinary method used by Mary

and Joseph, attack the problem, not the child or adult. To change someone else's present or possible future behavior:

a) Describe *how* you feel, by simply saying, "I feel ... "—anxious, afraid, worried, upset, concerned, sad, unhappy, disappointed, discouraged, etc.

b) Describe *what* caused you to feel as you do.

c) Describe *why* you feel as you do, giving the result or possible result of the behavior.

Children want explanations. Some ask, "Why?" because they want to understand. Explaining to a child *how* we feel, teaches the child how his words or actions affect others. Explaining *what* causes us to feel as we do, teaches him that his actions or words are not acceptable. Explaining *why* we feel as we do, teaches him the effect or possible effect of his unacceptable actions.

The *how-what-why* procedure eliminates using the word "you," which blames. *Love does not blame.* Blaming others causes hurt feelings and resentment. Mary, the mother of Jesus, expressed the problem in a non-blaming manner when she said to her son, "Your father and I have been anxiously (showing *how* they felt) searching for you" (telling *what* caused them to feel anxious). Observe that she did not say, "*You* caused us to be anxious," or "*You* caused us to waste three days of our time searching for you." She did not use the word "you" to blame him. She simply explained.

The *how-what-why* explanations can be used in all relationships. Following are other illustrations of the *how-what-why* procedure which does not blame:

Rather than saying, "You tracked up my clean floor with your muddy shoes" (blaming) say, "I am discouraged (*how* you feel); I just mopped the floor, and now it is dirty (*what* causes you to feel as you do), so I will have to mop it again" (*why* you feel as you do). Only one complete *how-what-why* explanation may be necessary. To say, "I just mopped the floor," would be sufficient warning to avoid repeating that unacceptable behavior in the future.

Rather than saying, "You be quiet," say, "I am afraid (*how* you feel) the noise will distract me from concentrating on my driving (*what* causes you to feel as you do), and we might have an accident which could hurt someone (*why* you feel as you do)." After the problem is once understood, in the event of a recurrence, a briefer explanation will be sufficient, such as "the noise is distracting me." Rather than saying, "You are driving too fast," say, "Driving fast makes me nervous," or give brief information, such as "The speed limit is fifty-five miles per hour."

In the event of immediate danger, when there is not enough time to use the complete *how-what-why* procedure, a very brief warning will be necessary. If a child is about to touch a hot object, the parent should say the word "Hot!" in a loud abrupt tone of voice. A wise parent will communicate with his child in a normal tone of voice, and will reserve loud and brief communication as a warning of immediate danger. The child will then be able to differentiate between immediate or less immediate danger and respond accordingly. After the child has been warned, and is heedful of the warning, the parent should explain that he could be hurt by oncoming cars, electrical outlets and other dangerous situations. Of course, a child who is not old enough to understand should have a "childproofed environment. How to "childproof" an environment is explained in the chapter **Love Protects**.

A father was walking on a city sidewalk with his young son beside him. The child began to run towards a highly-traveled intersection. The father, who normally spoke to the child in a soft voice, shouted the child's name. The child immediately stopped running. He sensed his father's warning of danger. (A small child who is not old enough to understand the meaning of danger should be held by the hand or by a special harness in dangerous situations). The father then explained to the child that he was afraid (*how* he felt) that the child could be hurt (*why* he was afraid) if he ran in front of an oncoming car (*what* caused the father to be afraid).

A volunteer who understood the value of the *how-what-why* procedure worked with social workers in a community center where male youth were carrying knives. They used the knives as a means of unkind power to control others just as their parents had used unkind power (hitting, slapping, spanking) to control them. The youths knew that threatening to use the knives gave them more power than the clout used by their parents. As a means of keeping the youth in this community constructively occupied after school hours, the community center provided classes in subjects which were of interest to them. The volunteer was to teach some of the classes and help supervise group activities. The volunteer knew from her study of human action and reaction that the youth would use the knives to threaten her if she, in any way, made them feel that she, the authority, would unkindly attack them. *She knew she had to express her problem rather than attack them.* A sewing class had been scheduled for the volunteer to teach. Both teenage boys and girls came to the class. The youth were quite boisterous. The volunteer teacher could not speak in a normal tone and still be heard above the noise. She knew that if she (the authority) attacked them in any way, they would resent her, and that could easily lead to more serious problems. After a few seconds of thought, the teacher said softly, "I cannot speak loudly enough to be heard by everyone." A student who was near her heard her words and bellowed to the others, "Quiet, so we can hear the teacher!" There was abrupt silence. The teacher spoke softly; they listened quietly. Occasionally, a youth would forget to be silent during class time, but there was always another youth who would remind him to be silent. *They disciplined themselves because they understood her problem.*

A word of caution. Never use the *how-what-why* procedure as a means of "putting down" a child or making him feel unacceptable. Words which convey the message, "I feel ashamed of you" or "You disappoint me" can devastate a child. Rather than attacking the child, attack the problem.

The adult or child who has been taught to obey rules out of the fear of punishment, may not respond to explanations (the *how-what-why* procedure) given to him. This is due to the fact that he is in the habit of obeying rules only when the threat of punishment is involved. A child may not respond to the *how-what-why* explanations if they are not properly executed. Also, he may not respond to the *how-what-why* procedure if the explanation is unreasonable, unnecessary or excessive.

The chapter **Love Is Not Rude** gives further information about the *how-what-why* procedure. The advantages of kind discipline are explained in the chapter **Self-Discipline, the Goal of Discipline**.

Love Is Unselfish

In Ephesians 5:21 (NIV), we read, "Submit to one another out of reverence for Christ." Also, Romans 12:16 (NIV) instructs man to "Live in harmony with one another." Surely God intended for parents to love their children and live in harmony with them.

An unselfish person cares about the feelings and well-being of others (including children).

An unselfish person makes decisions including others who are affected by the decision.

An unselfish person does not dominate another.

An unselfish person resolves conflicts in a compromising way, enabling everyone to feel satisfied. When one must have his way, the loser resents him: thus, love does not prevail. The one who gets his way becomes the selfish person at the expense of the unselfish one. Dr. Thomas Gordon, in *Parent Effectiveness Training*, page 194, refers to resolving conflicts in an unselfish manner as the "No-Lose" method for resolving conflicts.

A joint search for a compromise should be worked out by carefully listening to each other in an effort to understand each other's needs and viewpoints.

When listening, it is important:

1) Not to tune out what we do not want to hear.

2) Not to interpret in the way we want.

3) To have an open mind to an opposing or different viewpoint.

4) To avoid interrupting.

5) To discuss without anger—anger blocks open-mindedness and the ability to think rationally.

6) To clarify confusion by saying, "I don't understand."

7) To explain what we thought was meant to assure mutual understanding.

8) To listen to each other with mutual respect (this includes children).

9) For parents and children to work out solutions to resolve conflicting needs. Children learn from the parents' example and experiences shared with their parents. The knowledge and experience of resolving conflicts in an unselfish manner will be carried into adult behavior.

A compromise of needs can be worked out by the parent even with an infant. An infant crying from the fear of being alone and helpless can be made to feel secure by being near the parent. There are devices, such as infant carriers, which hold him close to the parent. Rocking devices, which can be put in the same room with the parent will give the infant a secure feeling as well as allowing the parent to assume his responsibilities; therefore, both parties are satisfied. A young toddler can satisfy his God-given curiosity for learning about his surroundings when his parents "child-proof" his environment; thus, both the child and parent are satisfied.

Following are some examples of how a parent can work out needs of the child and parent so that both are satisfied: The parent can explain to the child who can understand speech, "I am afraid that jumping on this good couch might ruin it, but there is an old mattress or jumping mat downstairs on which you may jump." "I am busy now but I will have time to read to you this evening." "Tonight we will have daddy's favorite food. Tomorrow night we will have your favorite food." "I am afraid this book will get torn, but you may have this magazine to play with."

As soon as a child is old enough to discuss and reason, encourage him to participate in a search for a compromise—a child who has learned to work out compromises with his parent will become an adult who will know how to work out conflicts in a peaceful, kind, unselfish and non-blaming manner. If our national leaders had learned how to work out unselfish and kind compromises as children (rather than force and unkind power to solve problems) wouldn't this be a more peaceful world?

When I go to the supermarket or toy store, I hear

many children and parents in disharmony with each other. I wish these parents and children could learn the system I adopted to avoid this unpleasant scene. As a result it has been a pleasure to go shopping with both my children and grandchildren. When children are small, they can ride in a grocery shopping cart. The parent can ask them to help find the items wanted by pointing to them. The parent can allow the children to pick one dessert, one meat, one fruit and one vegetable which they like. In so doing the adult includes the children, which avoids selfishness on the parent's part. Both parties are satisfied, which makes shopping more pleasurable.

At the age when children are learning to count, parents can give them a small allowance each week. As they grow older they can earn money by helping with simple jobs they can do with adults, such as picking up stones out of the lawn. (To command a small child to do a job by himself is futile. Children like to do what the adults are doing). A child's help is usually not perfect, but children cannot learn unless they are given the opportunity. Also, their interest span is short.

When children are old enough, an adult can help them count the money they save before they go shopping. During the shopping trip, when children want to buy nearly everything they see, it is necessary to explain that big folks cannot buy everything they see—they have to choose what is most important. Also, they must have the necessary amount of money to buy what they want. An adult can help the children relate the amount of money they have to the price of the object they chose. Sometimes they will realize that they cannot afford to buy a more expensive item and will settle for a less expensive one. (A very young child will not understand this procedure; therefore, it may be necessary to divert his attention when he wants something of which the parents do not approve).

I recall an incident with my three-year-old grand-daughter. She had decided that she wanted to buy a toy mouse. She saved her money until she thought she had enough. I had some shopping to do and took her with me. She was patient while I did my shopping—she knew that her turn would eventually come to go shopping for her mouse. She had learned that she must earn the amount of money she needed for her purchase, but she had not learned comparative shopping. To this objective, we decided to look in two different stores to see what kind of toy mice they sold and the cost. After we looked at wooden, glass and cloth mice in both stores, I asked her "Which one do you like best?" She chose the stuffed cloth mouse. I queried her as to why she didn't choose the glass mouse. She replied, "I might break it." Then I asked why she didn't choose the wooden mouse. She replied "It's too hard." Also, we had looked at the price tags while we were shopping and she added "I had only enough money to buy the cloth mouse." I was amazed that at the age of three she could reason so well. (Little minds can learn to reason if they are given the opportunity. However, children have different abilities).

Listening to Others Without Judgment

The Bible instructs man to "Confess your sins to each other and pray for each so that you may be healed" (James 5:16 NIV). Also, "Everyone should be quick to listen, slow to speak and slow to become angry" (James 1:19 NIV).

Jesus was an empathetic listener. He did not blame wrongdoers. He prayed so others could be healed.

Acceptance frees the speaker to share feelings, thoughts and problems with others (including children). We need to accept other's ideas even if we think they are wrong. Galations 6:2, instructs us to "Carry each others' burdens" (listening) which allows us to vent disappointments, fears, hurt and angry feelings; otherwise, these could become hostile and resentful feelings or worrisome tension.

Philippians 2:12-13 (NIV) tells us to "Work out your own salvation, for it is God who works in you to will and act according to his good purpose." The freedom to express feeling and thought helps in solving problems. It allows the person to concentrate on the problem rather than on his feeling of rejection and resentment. When we urge an adult or a child to push a feeling away, it becomes more upsetting. The non-empathetic listener gives the impression that he does not care about the feelings of others, which makes the speaker feel rejected.

An understanding person will listen without judgment. To give the advice "forget it" encourages repressed feelings which can become uncontrollable sub-conscious feelings causing emotional harm.

The act of acceptance gives the feeling that the speaker is loved and promotes a sense of self-worth and self-esteem. Children learn the communication of acceptance from the parent's example in dealing with them.

The best stress therapy involves talking about problems to an understanding person, prayer, physical exercise and relaxation therapy. Positive attitudes are helpful.

The head psychiatrist of the psychiatric unit at a large hospital asked a volunteer if she would like to work with him in an effort to help the mentally ill. He knew that she had studied and understood abnormal behavior, and was working as a volunteer in the recreational division of the psychiatric ward of the hospital. He explained that he had observed that she was sensitive to the patient's emotions, which gave her the ability to "pick up" clues of "bottled up" or repressed emotional problems. She was pleased to know that she could be helpful, so she accepted his invitation. She listened to reports of devastating and horrible abusiveness. She could relate to their feelings because she had experienced similar hurt, hopelessness, despair, anger and rejection from being unloved. Her empathy gave them the feeling that someone understood and cared about them. Some of the patients would tell her that they knew she cared because she was there as a volunteer. She also listened to some deeply-rooted fears that they were going to be punished by God.

Love Accepts Others

In Romans 15:7 (NIV) we read, "Accept one another just as Christ accepted you."

Family members need loving attention, affection and approval to feel they are accepted by others. *The use of unkind words and actions conveys rejection rather than acceptance.* A hug can convey acceptance in a way that words cannot.

Accept others (especially children) for their efforts. Too much emphasis on winning or being at the "top" can cause a defeatist attitude when a child or adult does not win or is not the best. Or the opposite may result. He may pressure himself beyond his natural capability in an effort to please others. This pressure can cause stress and emotional problems.

A grandmother attended an acrobatic event in which two of her granddaughters competed. After they had performed, both were near tears because they had not succeeded in being "perfect." The grandmother explained to them that she had come to the performance because she loved them—not because she expected them to win the competition. Also, the grandmother added that she knew they had done their best and one cannot do better than that.

Competitive activities are inclined to make some losers feel unacceptable. A better reason for participation in these events is the enjoyment and pleasure of doing them rather than putting so much emphasis on being the winner.

"Each of us should please others for his good, to build himself up" (Romans 15:2 NIV). Children, also, like to please others. To let the individual know that his efforts are pleasing, (acceptable), we should express our feelings or thoughts about what we see and hear, such as "Seeing such a clean and orderly room pleases me." That is kind of you." "You did your best."

The practice of giving family members a choice in making decisions which affect them will give them the feeling that they are accepted. Make a list of the pro's and con's of the decision to be made. Then consider both sides before the choice is made. Allow children, when they are old enough, to participate. This will also give them the opportunity to learn how to make decisions.

"A small word can corrupt a person. The same mouth can speak in appreciation or rejection" (James 3:3-12 NIV). A gossiper, who gossips as a means of putting a person down to build himself up, can corrupt others by making them feel they are not acceptable. A child often becomes what he is labelled—whether it be clumsy, dumb, irresponsible, kind, or other such attributes. Constant "put downs" can destroy children's self-confidence.

Corinthians 12:11 (NIV) states: "When I was a child, I talked like a child, I thought like a child, I reasoned like a child." Accept children for their God-given growing stages. Children have to go through these growing stages before they can employ mature adult behavior. An example is the toddler's curiosity. His need to get into and examine things is a means of learning about his new environment. He does not have the ability to "sit still" as adults do. Books on understanding childrens' growing stages are available in libraries. *Bringing Out the Best in Your Baby,* by Art Ulene and Steven Shelov, explains child development from birth to age four.

Accept the individual child for his unique abilities and interests. Parents should give children the opportunity to find their God-given talents rather than demanding what the parents desire for them. Some children have the coordination for sports, others do not. Some children have the ability to learn faster than others. Children within the same family are different. One child should not be compared with another. The practice of comparing children can be interpreted by a child as showing favoritism, which can cause jealousy and the feeling of being unacceptable. Encourage, stimulate and support the child's efforts by showing an interest in his abilities and interests. Express your approval by saying "I like the picture you made." "I am pleased that you like to learn to play the piano." "I am pleased with your progress." "I like watching you play baseball." Parental pressure, force or negative criticism often discourages (rather than encourages) the child's willingness to pursue his interest and talent.

Interest and talent can usually be categorized in four different forms. The ladder of success, self-fulfillment and contentment for careers and hobbies are listed in the following table:

Ladder of Success for Careers and Hobbies

	Ability or Talent	Interest	Potential for success	Self-fulfillment	Comments
(1)	Yes	Yes	High	High	Most desirable
(2)	No	Yes	High/Low	High/Low	A person can compensate for his lack of ability by the determination that his interest gives him.
(3)	Yes	No	High/Low	High/Low	With a lack of interest, a person usually has to pressure himself to succeed
(4)	No	No	Low	Low	A person who is forced by a parent or forces himself is least apt to be content and successful.

I have experienced all four of these combinations of talent and interest during my lifetime. (The numbers in the parentheses come from the previous table.)

1)   Both talent and interest—During my high school years, I realized that I did not have the God-given ability to memorize as well as some other classmates; therefore, I received low grades in the subjects that required a lot of memorization. However, my home economics teacher recognized that I had a talent and interest for color harmony, artistic design and creativity. She encouraged me to pursue this as a career.

4)   Neither talent nor interest—After I graduated from high school I wanted to attend college to study artistic design and interior decorating. My father's idea of a lady's occupation was to be a secretary. He gave me the choice of going to a business college or no college education at all. I chose to go to the business college. I studied shorthand, typing and all the subjects required to become a secretary, but my inability to memorize well and my lack of interest resulted in poor grades. I was at the point of giving up the struggle when . . .

3)   Talent but no interest—the president of the business college called me to his office and said that the teaching staff thought I had a talent for accounting, which would involve more reasoning than memorization. I then realized I had a God-given talent for thinking through situations and problems. That same college president (God bless him!) drove sixty miles in an old model-T Ford to my father's home to persuade him to allow me to switch to a major in accounting. I had the talent for accounting but not much interest; therefore, I knew I had to force myself to study. My grades in the new subjects

were good, and after receiving my accounting degree, I was offered two jobs as head accountant for large companies. I accepted the one I thought would be most interesting. The company I chose gave me an excellent starting salary and pay raises for good work. Also, they provided me with a personal bodyguard because my work involved top government secrets. As a businesswoman I could not have wished for more; but I did not have the interest in such a career, and forcing myself to stay with the position became stressful. I stayed with the job until my husband had earned his Ph.D. degree and was employed. Then, I had the good fortune to have a college nearby with an excellent program in the study of human action and reaction. The program required taking general psychology before taking other courses in which I was interested. The study of general psychology included learning the names of all the nerves in the body. I spent several hours a day in seemingly endless repetition in an effort to memorize the information. After I took the mid-semester test, I was pleasantly surprised to receive a good transcript. I had succeeded. It was the first time I had gotten a good grade when memorization was required. My interest overcame my low talent.

A problem arose as the result of earning A's for my effort. In 1946, the college I attended was a college for males. Females were allowed to attend classes and receive credit for the courses taken but were not allowed to do a thesis for a degree. My second semester transcript was also excellent. A group of male students, who were working for degrees, approached me and asked if I would take the courses for no-credit since they knew I was not eligible for a degree. At the time, letter grades were determined by a curve at that college. The highest grade received an A, which I had received. This meant that the students who were getting D's and F's would have had a higher grade if it had not been for my A grades. A group of male students asked me to audit the classes rather than take them for credit so they could have better grades. To please them I audited the future classes. This eliminated my potential for earning a degree in psychology, but I put my knoweldge to good use working as a volunteer in this field. Also, I learned how to discipline my children in an understanding and loving manner, which was my objective.

Love Rejoices in the Truth

It is normal for younger children to fantasize. They enjoy make-believe stories, books and play. The parents can explain to a child that this is a make-believe story or this is a real story, especially in television viewing. It may be difficult for parents to distinguish between his child's fantasy and real stories. A wise parent will not reprimand his child for his childish behavior. If parents are concerned about Santa Claus stories, they can explain to the child that we pretend Santa Claus has a sleigh with reindeer and he comes down the chimneys.

The untruth can be told as the result of misunderstanding, misinterpretation and jumping to conclusions without knowing all the facts. The chapter **Love is Unselfish** tells how to carefully listen in an effort to communicate the truth.

Adults and children deliberately lie to avoid punishment or disapproval. A teen-age boy knew his parents did not approve of his dating girls. They did not want him to be alone with a girl. The boy told his parents that he was going to stay with a male friend overnight. While there, he went on a date with a girl, unbeknown to his parents. Undoubtedly, the boy would not have lied to his parents if his parents had practiced working out differences in a compromising way. The parents could have invited the girl to their home, driven them to the movies, or worked out another solution that would have satisfied the needs of both parties. *Learning to lie to avoid punishment or disapproval can become a habit. Learning to work out compromises is a better habit to learn.*

It is unwise to make a promise unless the promise can be fulfilled. Children learn to lie from their parents' example.

A negative criticism usually can be stated in a positive way. Rather than saying, "I don't like this casserole," say, "I liked the casserole you made last week better," or "I prefer meat and potatoes."

The person who deliberately lies causes others to lose trust and faith in him; thus, love does not prevail. A person loses trust and faith in the hypocrite who pretends to have moral beliefs and principles which he does not have.

In James 3:5-7 (NIV), we read about taming the tongue. "Consider what a great forest is set afire by a small spark. The tongue also is a fire, a world of evil among the parts of the body. It corrupts the whole person, sets the whole course of his life on fire, and is itself set on fire by hell." When we indulge in tearing others down to build ourselves up or blame others to relieve ourselves of wrongdoing, we can corrupt the whole person.

Love Is Patient and Slow to Anger

The practice of patience gives others (including children) time to adjust to a change. Saying "Dinner will be ready in fifteen minutes" gives time to finish or bring an activity to a stopping point. To demand an immediate change can cause resentment or frustration which can lead to tantrums in young children.

A person who learns to be patient avoids irritation for himself as well as for those whom he may irritate as the result of his impatience.

The habit of being impatient can be learned from parental example.

The lack of understanding and acceptance of individual differences can result in impatience.

The act of impatience can be induced by expecting too much of a child or not understanding children's growing stages.

The lack of understanding parent action and child reaction can be a cause of impatience. Human action and reaction is explained in the chapter **Biblical Love in Action**.

Stress can add to the problem of being impatient. The book *Controlling Stress and Tension* by Daniel Girdano and George Everly explains the causes of stress and various techniques for relaxation and attitudes to help overcome stress and tension.

Love Is Not Jealous or Possessive

All children are God's children. Only God's power can create a child. The parent's purpose in a child's life is to nurture, to love and to give him the freedom to grow into adult life as an individual, each day becoming more independent of his parent.

Children and adults are meant to be loved, not to be possessed by parents or spouses. Parents or spouses who are jealous and possessive usually were emotionally deprived of love in their earlier years.

Jealousy is emotionally destructive. A jealous person sometimes has the need to compete with the person of whom he is jealous. Or, he may indulge in degrading or hurting the person of whom he is envious.

If a parent is possessive of a child, especially an only child, and then grows jealous of the person whom the child marries, an emotionally destructive atmosphere is created. In one case, after an only child was married, the mother chose to live with her son and daughter-in-law. The possessive and jealous mother-in-law said to the new daughter-in-law, "I will get even with you for taking my son away from me." The daughter-in-law knew the mother-in-law as a kind and loving parent to her son. Her unkind need to get even with her was confusing for the new daughter-in-law. It would take pages to write of the problems the mother-in-law deliberately created for her daughter-in-law. The daughter-in-law went into a state of depression because she could not cope with her mother-in-law's unkindness. Finally, the couple sought psychiatric help. The psychiatrist advised the son to find another home for his mother, which he did. The daughter-in-law rarely saw her husband's mother after that. He would frequently visit his mother without his wife. During those visits, the woman felt that she had her son all to herself. She was content with this arrangement.

During the time I was supervising a church nursery school, the minister asked if I would accept a four-year old child whose mother suddenly died. I learned that this only child had no opportunities outside his home. His mother had evidently been possessive and kept him entirely for herself. He now had no one to take care of him except his father. He was completely devastated and frightened, not knowing that others could care for him. He had not played with other children nor had the experience of attending a nursery school. The father delivered his motherless son to our nursery school. The boy was the most distraught and frightened child I have ever known. The environment and everyone was completely strange to him. He sobbed and cried continuously, asking for his mother. The only thing I could think of to help him was to hold him. I did this for nearly two months. The other nursery children asked why I held him and not them. I explained that they had mothers to hold them, but he did not have a mother to hold him. They seemed to be satisfied with the explanation. After about two months, he began to watch the other children play. He did not know how to relate to them. Finally, he would sit by himself and play with clay and paints. He would watch the others but did not want to play with them. The school year ended. I do not know what happened to him after that. The boy would have been better able to cope with the sudden change in his life if his mother had encouraged more socialization in her son. Simply allowing others to care for him from time to time, would have made the adjustment to the loss of his mother easier.

Love Is Not Rude

Grabbing objects from a child (or any other person) is rude. A mother, who had the habit of grabbing objects from her children, thoughtlessly grabbed a sharp knife from her young son. She was afraid he might hurt himself with the knife. As the mother pulled the knife through the child's hand, she severely cut it. The mother should have held out her hand and said, "I am afraid you might hurt yourself with the knife—please give it to me." If a child is too young to understand a verbal request, then the parent should slowly and carefully remove an object from the child.

The use of rude, unexplained commands, such as, "Don't do that," "Stop that" and "Shut up" convey rejection and hurtful feelings. Also, these commands do not explain the reason for the command.

I was visiting a family at their home. As I was sitting on their porch overlooking a beautiful view, I said to the father of the family, "What a beautiful view!" The father rudely said to me, "Stop that." I was bewildered. I had not said or done anything that was offensive. I felt rejected and hurt. Without saying another word, I went to my car to think about my problem. I remembered that someone had said that the father had difficulty hearing. I realized that perhaps he was annoyed because I was not speaking loudly enough. I returned to the porch where he was sitting and said in a loud voice, "You have a beautiful view." He reacted with a smile. In this instance, the father could have said to me "I am sorry, I cannot hear you (*expressing his problem*) rather than attacking me with the rude and unexplained words, "Stop that."

As revealed in Luke 2:48, Mary, the mother of Jesus, did not use a rude command, such as, "Don't do that again." If a command is necessary, it should be given in a kind manner, such as, "I need the hammer; would you please get it for me?" rather than to rudely command, "Go get the hammer." To give information is kinder than a rude command. To say, "The pan is hot" (giving information) is kinder than rudely commanding, "Don't touch that pan." To say, "The grass needs mowing" (giving information) is kinder than giving a rude command, "Go mow the grass." The use of vulgar words (which I will not mention) is offensive and rude.

Children learn to relate to others in the manner in which their parents deal with them—in a rude manner or a non-rude manner.

Love Protects

A part of loving others is protecting them from emotional and physical harm. Children want protection but not overprotection.

Infants and young children who cannot communicate their problems and needs by speech use crying and other types of behavior in an effort to communicate with the parent. It may be helpful to use the elimination method in an effort to find an infant's problem. For instance, change his diaper; if he continues to cry, try giving him food. He may be too warm or cold. If that does not solve the problem, perhaps he needs to be held close to the parent for a secure or warm feeling. If none of these actions have satisfied his need, then think about the possibility that he may be suffering from a more serious discomfort, such as gas, cutting teeth, other pain or illness.

It is a proven fact that the lack of cuddling and holding of a small child close to an adult can cause serious emotional and physical problems. Holding and cuddling a child *does not spoil him*—it gives him the feeling of being loved and secure, which he needs for good emotional health. It has been observed that children who are deprived of affection and attention become adults who have an excessive need for attention and affection. This is seen in youths' need for early sex and in adult illicit affairs, which are efforts to satisfy a subconscious need for attention and affection.

When we hit (spank) children, or when we are tense, we can cause children to fear us. Children, especially young children, quickly sense our tension, which frightens them. Tension can become an endless cycle of the child crying from the fear of our tension, or being hurt by us, while we, in turn, become more tense and unkind with the child. A pediatrician whom I knew said, "I give tranquilizers to the parents of a child who is suffering from tension, rather than to the child."

How to help the young child adjust to unfamiliar people and environment is discussed in *Bringing Out the Best in Your Baby,* by Art Ulene, M.D. and Steven Shelov, M.D. The book explains the following:

1) The age the young child begins to become fearful that his parent will not return when the parent leaves him.

2) The symptoms of fear.

3) How to help the young child adjust to parent separation without causing a traumatic event for the child.

God gave human beings the feeling of sleepiness when the body requires sleep. Each individual (including children) has different requirements. Small children require less sleep as they grow older. A child will fall alseep when he needs sleep if he is relaxed; therefore, bed and nap time should be pleasant and relaxed occasions. The parent can rock him, read to him, tell him a story, or rub his back as means of helping him relax if the child is upset or over-excited. The time the parent spends with the child gives a feeling of security, and added inducement for peaceful sleep.

Children quickly sense their parent's rejection of them when they are forced to go to bed as a means for the parent to relieve himself of the responsibility of caring for the child. This forcing and rejection causes tension, which results in sleep problems.

It has been observed that some parents force their children to go to bed because they, the parents, are sleepy. This also causes unpleasantness, which is then associated with going to bed and, in turn, causes tension.

Putting a child to bed as a means of punishment causes an unpleasant association with going to bed. This causes tension and the inability to sleep well.

Some physical reasons can cause sleeping problems. A parent should discuss these with a physician.

A parent should not attempt to potty train a child until he is sufficiently mature and capable of controlling this function. Some children master this task later than others. Forced training before individual maturity can cause problems. Problems should be discussed with a physician.

To verbally protect a child from physical harm, use the words "Johnny fell," "Johnny got hurt," or "hot" when he falls, gets hurt, or experiences the feeling of something hot. He will then learn to associate the words with what is happening to him. Use these words, in a loud voice if necessary, when he is about to encounter one of these dangers. If the child knows what might happen to him, usually he will willingly employ self-discipline and heed his parent's warning without being forced to do so. In the event of immediate danger, a more brief action may be necessary, such as grasping the child.

The word "no" does not tell the child what he is about to encounter as effectively as the words "fall," "hurt" or "hot" do. The parent who constantly bellows the word "no" to discipline the child will have a child who will bellow the word "no" in his relationship with his parents. If the parent punishes the child for following his (the parent's) example of using the word "no," then the child will become confused and frustrated because the parent has employed a double standard of behavior. Children who are frustrated release their frustration by the use of tantrums. They become frustrated when their needs are opposed by the parents' needs. Tantrums should be ignored. The child will soon learn that tantrums are not the way to solve his problem. However, the parent should learn to work out his child's needs and his own needs in a compromising way to avoid selfishness on the part of the child or parent. (See chapter **Love Is Unselfish**). Giving a warning before a change of activity, such as "We will be going home soon," and assuring the child that he can return to his activity, such as "You can play with your doll tomorrow," can help to avoid frustration. Diverting the child's attention helps in peacefully removing the child from an undesirable situation, object or activity.

It has been observed that toddlers who were not allowed to explore a "child-proofed" environment had a decreased incentive for learning, which later negatively affected their school work. These children became adults who did not have the curiosity which gives the incentive for interest and accomplishment in science, medicine and other related fields.

It has also been observed that children who were allowed to examine their environment had the incentive to learn and became good students. A large portion of these students went into science, medicine and occupations that required the sense of curiosity to maintain interest and success.

I spanked my first toddler for running into the street. He ran into the street again. Fortunately, he did not get injured. It was I who had to learn that spanking may or may not teach right from wrong. I also realized that it was necessary to provide a *protective environment to preserve my child's life.* Outdoor play areas for small children should be surrounded by a protective fence. Indoor areas should be "child-proofed." That is, dangerous and breakable objects should be removed from the child's reach. Also, gates, drawer catches and other protective devices should be used for a young child's protection until he is old enough to understand and respond to parental verbal instruction and explanations.

A mother spanked her child for running into the street. Over and over the child ran in front of traveling cars and each time the mother spanked the child, until he was nearly five years old. Fortunately, the cars were going slowly enough to stop before they hit the child. An adult friend was quite concerned for his life. Therefore, she took the child to a street corner. She asked the child, "What should we do before we cross the street?" He replied, "Run." The friend asked the child, "What should we do before we run across the street?" He looked at her with a bewildered look. She then realized that he had not been taught to look in both directions before he crossed the street. His impression of getting across the street safely was to run as fast as he could go. The friend immediately taught him to look in both directions for oncoming cars. She asked him to tell her when it was safe to cross the street. And so he did. They walked a block to the next street crossing. She said nothing. The child looked in both directions. She asked, "Can we go now?" He replied, "Yes." They crossed the street and walked to the next street crossing. Again, the friend said nothing. The child looked in both directions and the friend followed him. She observed that he continued to look for oncoming cars after her instruction. *The child learned to cross the street safely from kind instruction.*

Provide a variety of activities for the child; however, do not force a child to engage in activities which do not appeal to him. Forcing usually discourages rather than encourages. If the activity is necessary, try to make it interesing.

To dominate (to constantly control others) with a continuous flow of commands, such as "Eat your food!" "Eat your vegetables!" "Drink your milk!" "Go to bed!" "Go to sleep!" "Go to the bathroom!" can cause the following problems:

1)   Resentment of the domination, thus causing disobedience. For example, a child who is dominated at the dinner table often will become a problem eater. It has been observed that children who are not allowed to eat sweet foods when they were served on the dinner table, often sneak them when the parent is not around. It is far better not to have these foods continually available;

reserve them for special occasions. This avoids addiction to the sugar in sweet foods. A child usually will eat a balanced diet over a period of a week if he has not been forced. However, if there is concern about the child's eating habits, the parents should consult their physicians.

2)   To dominate may cause a child to "tune out" or ignore all instruction because he cannot differentiate between what is most important and not so important if there are too many commands, unimportant rules, and expectations.

3)   To dominate a child may deprive him of his ability to learn to assume responsibilities for himself. For example, doing his homework without being told to do it. He becomes dependent on the nagging.

Most children know the difference between reasonable and unreasonable restrictions. Unreasonable restriction can cause anger and thus the "battleground." Some unreasonable restrictions can be the result of parents not understanding the child's growing stages. For example: During the teen-age years the child develops the God-given need to grow independent of the parent. The parent who tries to restrict his child from growing independent, and does not allow the child to employ self-discipline, can create a "battleground." To restrict the young child's curiosity about exploring and examining a harmless environment can cause a "battleground."

It has been observed that younger children are prone to "set up" older children as a means of competing for attention. A five-year old boy had built a house with his construction toys. The younger three-year old sister deliberately knocked her brother's house down. The brother (who had been disciplined with hitting) hit his sister. The younger sister went crying to her mother explaining, "Johnny hit me." Of course, Johnny was punished, and his sister given sympathy and affection— she had successfully gained the favor of the parent.

A subject of concern in today's society is depression and teen-age suicide. Many parents do not recognize the symptoms of depression and suicide. Depression can occur at any age.

Childhood depression can be the result of:

1) Lack of discipline which is non-dominating, reasonable, kind, un-selfish, non-blaming and protective.

2) Constant negative criticism or "put-downs."

3) Pressuring the child to engage in activities that the parent wants for the child, rather than allowing the child to follow his own abilities and interests.

4) Parental or school expectations which are too high or difficult for the child to achieve.

5) Feeling unloved or unacceptable.

6) Loss of (or separation from) a loved one or animal.

7) Lack of comunication, of having someone listen.

8) Lack of parental quality (loving) time spent with the child.

9) School, teacher and friend problems.

10) Other stressful problems.

11) Physical problems.

Coping With Teenage Depression by Kathleen McCoy discusses the symptoms and causes of depression and suicide. The book also lists low-cost individual and family counseling throughout the United States and Canada.

Self-Discipline, the Goal of Discipline

The English word "discipline" is derived from the Latin word "discipulus" meaning one who is taught or one who is learning. The English word "disciple" is also derived from the word "discipulus" (a person who teaches). The scripture Proverbs 22:6 (NIV) instructs parents to "Train up a child in the way he should go, and when he is old, he will not part from it."

The goal of discipline should be to teach and encourage self-discipline, for the good of all people and their property. When an adult or child does not see the reason for a rule, or why something is wrong, he will not see the need to obey the rule or change the action. Seeing the need to change, or obey a rule, influences him to employ self-discipline. For instance, an adult obeys the speed limit when driving, knowing it is for safety reasons.

An individual can also learn self-discipline from the natural experiences of his daily life. I recall when my toddler child touched a hot pan. His natural reflexes caused him to remove his finger quickly from the source of pain. At the moment he experienced the feeling, I said the word "hot" so he would learn to associate the feeling with the word. He soon learned that when I gave the warning "hot," he knew what to expect and would heed my brief warning. At that time, and throughout his entire childhood, he willingly heeded explained warnings.

The use of logical consequences can be helpful in teaching self-discipline when there is a constant problem. For instance, a child who constantly dawdles when dressing for an event such as a party with a precise starting time, can be left behind; however, a child should not be left alone.

At the time I was the supervisor of a nursery school, a boy who had the habit of "tuning out" his dominating parent's instruction also tuned out my instruction. Rather than making a special effort to get his attention day after day, I decided to use the logical consequence method of discipline. I knew he especially liked to see movies. I had announced to the class that we were going to another room to see a movie. All the children went to the room except the boy who, predicatably, "tuned out" my instruction. I allowed him to sit in the nursery alone with an assistant teacher. When the child realized that he had been left behind, the assistant teacher explained to him that I had announced "movie time," but apparently he had not heard it. I was amazed at how well he listened to my instruction after that experience.

In some circumstances, when self-discipline is not practiced, other means of correction can be more effective than punishment. In one community in New York State, the police are taking intoxicated drivers who have injured others in an automobile accident to the hospital emergency room to see the injured victim. The offender sees the pain and injury he has caused. He is also taken to the morgue to view a dead victim of an accident, and asked, "How would you feel if the deceased was someone you loved?" The police, however, are sensitive to the offender's reaction so as not to completely devastate him. It has been observed that this method of correction is more effective than putting the offender in a jail, where he does not face the reality of his actions.

The advantages of kindly teaching self-discipline, in the manner Jesus was taught, are as follows:

1)   Kindly teaching self-discipline eliminates learning unkind behavior from the parent's example of using unkind actions or words to discipline.

2)   It eliminates resentment of unkind action during discipline, which may cause subsequent unwilling cooperation, rebellion or retaliation.

3)   Kindly teaching self-discipline eliminates the need to lie, blame others, manipulate, or tattle to avoid punishment. Observe how many sins are committed as the result of wanting to avoid punishment. Matthew 18:6, Luke 17:2 and Mark 9:42, reveal that Jesus said, "Whoever causes one of these little ones who believe in me to sin, it would be better for him to have a great millstone fastened round his neck and drowned in the depth of the sea." Children who learn to lie (to avoid punishment) often become adults who lie; therefore, the threat of punishment can cause "one of these little ones to sin." To discipline in the manner Jesus was disciplined eliminates this problem.

4)   Kindly teaching self-discipline eliminates "policing" as a means of enforcing desirable behavior, especially in older children and adults. An example of adult misconduct when authority is not around to "police" them is speeding while using the so-called "fuzz-buster" to detect police radar. It is an electronic device used so a driver exceeding the speed limit can slow

down to the legal speed limit while in the neighborhood of the police to avoid being cited for speeding. He has no thought that the speed limit was set to protect the speedster, and others, from possible injury or death. In many cases, if these disobedient adults had learned self-discipline, realizing that rules are for the good of all people, they would not disobey laws when authority is not around to "police" them.

A two-year old child was punished for touching a breakable object. The child learned not to touch the object when the parent was present to "police" him. But immediately after the parent had left the house, the child was seen holding the forbidden object. (In this instance, the breakable object should have been put out of the child's reach until he was old enough to understand that the object was breakable).

5)   Kindly teaching self-discipline eliminates the fear of punishment as a means of discipline. Fear creates anxiety. Anxiety caused nervous tension. Tension results in many physical and emotional problems, such as the inability to sleep, a sick stomach, and other problems. Unkind punishment conveys rejection.

6)   Kindly teaching self-discipline encourages the God-given ability to reason; that is, to obey rules and distinguish right from wrong because one understands the reason for such.

7)   Kindly teaching self-discipline, by expressing *how* actions and words affect others, teaches concern for the feelings of others. Children who have been unkindly disciplined with unexplained feelings are inclined to become "hard hearted" adults who have little concern for the feelings of others.

8)   Kindly teaching self-discipline, that is, developing the ability to distinguish right from wrong and the consideration of the pro's and the con's of a situation before acting or speaking, eliminates acting or speaking impulsively.

9)   Kindly teaching self-discipline eliminates the inability to make decisions. A child who has usually had decisions made for him (when he is old enough to make decisions) will not be capable of considering the pro's and con's of an action. Parents who continually discipline a child with unexplained commands deprive the child of his God-given ability to reason for himself. Mary and Joseph did not use unexplained commands to discipline their son Jesus. They expressed the problem Jesus had created for them, and He, in turn, did not repeat his unacceptable behavior because He obviously understood the problem He had created for his parents.

10)   Kindly teaching self-discipline eliminates being influenced by the pressures or commands of the *un*desirable actions of peers. Children who have been taught to obey authority indiscriminately are inclined to respond to the *un*desirable pressures and commands of peers. They have not been allowed to defend or stand up for themselves. These are the children who have been known to give in to peer pressure involving sex, drugs, alcohol, cults, riding with a person who speeds, or engaging in other harmful actions.

11)   Kindly teaching self-discipline discourages the development of narrow-mindedness. Youth and adult narrow-mindedness is usually the result of authority having demanded rigid conformity to unexplained commands during childhood. Encouraging a child to

reason, to see right from wrong for himself by giving explanations promotes broad-mindedness and open-mindedness toward accepting new concepts and ideas. The child will then become an adult who will listen, consider others' advice, accept others' points of view and take instruction without feeling resentful. For instance, when a speeder is fined for exceeding the speed limit, he knows the law is for a safety reason; therefore, he will not be resentful of enforcement.

12)   Kindly teaching self-discipline eliminates low self-esteem which was brought about by negative criticism, "put down" or unkind actions in disciplining.

13)   It eliminates depression resulting from dominating, nagging, unreasonable, unkind, selfish or blaming discipline.

14)   It eliminates the typical "battling" with parents, especially during the teen-years.

15)   Kindly teaching self-discipline eliminates the fear of punishment, *which can be the cause of death.* A grandmother noticed that some of her heart medication was missing. She asked her grandchild if he had taken the pills. The child denied he had done so (he was afraid he would be punished for his action). Therefore, no medical treatment was immediately administered. The child revealed that he was afraid to admit he had taken the medication after it was too late to save his life. An autopsy verified that the child had taken the medication.

My brother died at the age of eight because he and I were afraid that our father would punish us if we complained that my brother was ill. (See the chapter **Children, Obey Your Parents in the Lord** for further details).

16)   Kindly teaching self-discipline eliminates the severe problems caused by severe, unkind discipline. These problems are listed in the chapter **A Great Error in Bible Interpretation**.

My husband and I disciplined our children with the principles of Biblical love and I can truly say from our experience that children so raised are willing to obey non-dominating, reasonable, kind, unselfish and non-blaming instruction and correction.

I recall overhearing a conversation between our oldest son, then age twelve, and a friend, whom I shall call Jack. Jack and our son were playing football in our back yard. Both the boys had soiled their jeans in play. Jack said to our son, "I am afraid to go home with these dirty jeans—my mother will kill me." Our son replied, "My mother will understand—she will wash them for you." Their conversation continued about their respective mothers attitudes. Jack's remarks concerning his mother were definitely not respectful. Our son expressed his attitude towards his mother with the words, "When my mom suggests that I do something, I know it is for my own good." I was surprised to hear that statement. I had not verbally told him to listen to my explanations for his own good. This was entirely his deduction.

At the age of two, our younger son would occasionally wreck his older brother's construction toys. I explained to the older child that his brother was too young to comprehend the fact that he was being destructive; therefore, we would have to find a way to solve the problem. After some thought and discussion, the older son decided that he would play with his construction toys while his younger brother was taking his nap, or go into a room by himself and close the door while his younger brother played in the kitchen with his toys, during the time I was preparing the evening meal. The situation was worked out in an unselfish way so both were satisfied, which avoided one getting his way at the expense of the loser. This procedure is explained in the chapter, **Love is Unselfish**. I recall another incident when we worked out a situation peacefully and there was no selfishness involved. Our older son and I were playing a game of checkers. The younger son wanted to get into the game, but he was not old enough to understand the rules. After some thought, I suggested that the younger move the checkers to where the older and I wanted them to be moved. By involving him in this way, the younger was delighted that he, too, could participate. Usually, younger children's span of interest is shorter than that of older children, and that was the case with our two. The younger one played only a short time and returned to toys more appropriate to his age level.

As our sons grew older they learned to resolve their differences by themselves, in the same unselfish manner we used in keeping peace between them during their younger years. Our children were always a joy to us, even in their teen-age years. When I hear parents complaining about their children or see them in disharmony with one another, I wish that they, too, could have learned how to relate to their children with the principles of Biblical love. As I look back, I cannot recall a time when our boys hit or physically fought with each other to solve their problems. Their disagreements were usually solved in a verbal, unheated manner. (I cannot say that about my brothers and me. I recall hitting and yelling in anger. Now, I realize we were copying our adult example of behavior in dealing with us.)

A Great Error in Bible Interpretation

The New Testament advised man to "Hate what is evil ... Do not repay anyone evil for evil ... Overcome evil with good [kind, unselfish and non-blaming action]" (Romans 12:9, 17, 21 NIV). Hating evil (wrongdoing) is a God-given emotion, but the scriptures instruct man to react to evil and correct wrongdoing with good.

One of the greatest errors in interpreting the Bible is in regard to the use of the word "rod."

The following is the explanation of the word "rod" as offered by Dr. Billy Graham and Rev. John Evans in a letter to the author:

> The word "rod" had various uses and connotations in ancient times. In the life of Moses and Aaron it was an emblem of authority (Exodus 4:2 and Numbers, Chapter 17). Psalm 2:9 speaks of the rod of Christ. Christ will either rule with the pastoral rod of the shepherd as described in Psalm 23, or He will break with the rod of iron (Isaiah 9:4; Revelation 2:27, 19:15)

In Verse 4 in the Twenty-Third Psalm, we read, "Thy rod and Thy staff, they comfort me." "Rod," as used in this verse, certainly does not mean an object to inflict physical pain. One would expect *comfort* as a result of God's kind guidance and correction, *not pain*. The word "rod" is also used in Proverbs 13:24: "He who spares the rod hates his son, but he who loves him is careful to discipline him." (The English word "discipline" comes from the Latin word "discipulus" meaning one who is taught or one who is learning.) "He who spares the 'rod'" in this text should also be interpreted as "He who spares giving *kind guidance and correction (not spare hurting the child)*."

Shepherds use the rod and staff in guiding sheep. When an obstacle is placed in front of traveling sheep, the sheep will turn in the direction of open space where there is no obstacle. Long sticks (rod and staff) held and stretched out beyond the arm's length of the sheepherder give the appearance of an obstacle; thus, the shepherd can direct the sheep properly in a kind yet controlled manner. The sheep will move forward with the shout of words such as "shoo, shoo," or with the gentle nudge of a stick (rod). The curve in the staff is used to catch the sheep around the neck. When a sheep is painfully struck by a shepherd, the sheep will flee in any direction (including the wrong direction) to get away from the source of pain. Often, other sheep will follow the fleeing sheep in the incorrect direction; thus, the shepherd loses control of his flock as the result of unkind guidance.

The use of the "rod" (inflicting pain) to correct wrongdoing is in direct opposition to the Biblical teaching to correct wrongdoing with kind actions. In fact, it is an attempt to correct wrongdoing (evil) with evil.

The passage Luke 2:41-52, reveals that Jesus was disciplined with kind verbal explanations rather than the use of the "rod" to inflict pain. There is no statement in the Bible which indicates that He was disciplined (taught) with a "rod" in an unkind manner. Nor is it mentioned that Jesus advised parents to use the "rod" (inflict pain) to discipline their children. Jesus commanded that we love one another. 1 Corinthians 13 defines love as kind. Jesus did *not* command us to be kind to adults and unkind to children. As an adult, the only time He laid his hand on anyone was to heal, not to hurt. He also corrected wrong-doing with verbal communication rather than punishment. Surely God intended for parents to love their children and obey the rules of love (as described in 1 Corinthians) in dealing with children as well as adults.

Effects of Unkind Discipline

When we use the "rod"-to-inflict-pain attitude (spanking or hitting) in dealing with a child, he is apt to follow our attitude and use hitting, kicking and bullying in his relationships with others, especially with younger children. Often, we will blame and reprimand the child for his unkind behavior, not realizing the child is following our unkind example. If we further use slapping and spanking to reprimand the child for hurting others, the child will get the idea that unkind action (hitting) is the only way to relate to others or solve problems. Or, he may withdraw from others because he does not know how to act. (This conflicting standard of morals can cause confusion.) These children can become depressed. Other problems which unkind discipline can cause are listed later in this chapter.

When we discipline in the kind manner in which Jesus was disciplined, we set a kind Christ-like example for children to follow, and thereby eliminate the many problems which unkind discipline causes.

Following is an instance of a mother who did not realize her young daughter followed her (the mother's) example of hitting. A music instructor at a summer music school and her three-year-old daughter paused to speak to a teen-age student. The instructor's child hit the student for no apparent reason other than the child had the idea that hitting was the way to relate to others. Obviously, the mother had not realized that her child had formed the idea of hitting others from her example of spanking the child. As the result of not understanding that the child was following her example, the mother instructed her young daughter to say to the student, "I'm sorry." The child stood speechless, undoubtedly, bewildered and confused, rather than obeying her mother's command. (It was obvious that the mother did not realize that she was creating a confusing double standard of morals for her young daughter by setting the example of hitting the child, then demanding that the child apologize for following the mother's example). Since the child did not obey the mother's command to say, "I'm sorry," the mother spanked her child. The child cried as the result of being emotionally and physically hurt. The child continued to cry. The mother spanked the child the third time. The child then said, "I'm sorry." If this mother had known how to discipline her child in the kind manner in which Jesus was disciplined, the child's as well as the mother's non-Christ-like actions could have been avoided.

To advise a parent to use the "rod" to inflict pain or discipline may be likened to advising a person to use alcohol. Some will know the disadvantages of its use, and refrain from using it, or use it sparingly. Others will use it to the point of causing emotional and physical harm. In Luke 17:1-3 (NIV), we read: "Jesus said to his disciples: 'Things that cause people to sin are bound to come, but woe to that person through whom they come. It would be better for him to be thrown into the sea with a millstone tied around his neck than for him to cause one of these little ones to sin. So watch yourselves.'" Authorities who use the "rod" or advise the use of the rod in an unkind way for discipline, are usually *unaware* that they are instilling the unchristian attitude that unkind actions are the way to resolve problems, teach right from wrong, or correct wrongdoing.

The following example shows the result of excessive spanking.

In 1952, the officials of a Methodist church supported me in establishing, supervising, and teaching a Christian nursery school. I recognized this as an opportunity to teach and employ the principles of Biblical love in disciplining children.

I requested that the parents of the pupils serve as assistant teachers. I wrote a pamphlet for them to study so they, too, could relate to the children in the same kind manner I had learned from my study of child behavior and nursery school procedures.

It became known that I was interested in children with emotional problems. The minister of the church asked me if I would accept an excessively spanked and emotionally disturbed child whom he knew. I was pleased to be given the opportunity to help the child. The child was being raised by his Christian grandmother who firmly believed in the use of the "rod to inflict pain" attitude for disciplining her grandchild. The grandmother expected the child to act as an adult. She spanked him for behaving as a normal child. The child followed his grandmother's example of spanking in the form of hitting and kicking. It became a cycle of the grandmother spanking the child, the child hitting and kicking the grandmother. The minister and I discussed the problem. We decided the grandmother probably would not change her attitudes; therefore, it would be best to separate them by inviting the child to attend our nursery school.

On the day the three-year old child arrived, I greeted him. He responded by kicking me. He hit the other children. The assisting teacher said to me, "He needs a good spanking." I explained that spanking was the cause of his problem—we should set an example of kindness rather than unkindness in dealing with him. The child kicked my legs every time I went near him, but I ignored his action. To prevent him from hitting or kicking the other children, I gave him special attention by reading to him. Also, I gave him activities of interest to him which did not involve the others. Slowly, he began to overcome some of his need to kick and hit.

At the age of five, the child attended kindergarten. I was concerned for his welfare. I called his teacher and explained his background and how we were trying to help him. She, too, tried to be helpful. I followed his progress through his years of school, and eventually he graduated from high school. He was married, but soon after his marriage, his wife divorced him on the grounds of physical abuse. He had great difficulty in assuming the responsibility of holding jobs, and also found that he was unable to get along peacefully with others. In spite of our efforts to set a kind example for the nursery school child to follow, we did not completely overcome the effect of his unkind parenting.

Angry feelings are normal; however, anger should be used in a constructive rather than a destructive manner. Spanking or hitting a child in anger may be a release for our angry feelings but the undesirable effects of emotionally and physically hurting the child are far out-reaching.

If we must punish a child, putting him in his room and telling him that he can come out when he feels ready to cooperate, eliminates the undesirable effects of spanking or hitting (Spock and Rothenberg 408).

Disciplined with unkindness and selfishness, children:

1) feel angry, unloved, unacceptable, lacking in self-esteem.

2) are taught to fear and hate authority.

3) feel justified in hitting smaller children because their parents set the example of hitting them (Spock and Rothenberg 408).

4) learn to lie to avoid punishment or disapproval.

5) do as they please when authority is not around to police them.

6) cannot be reasoned with because the parents set the example of hitting rather than reasoning to discipline them.

7) often run away because they cannot cope with parental unkindness and selfishness.

8) often join cults or undesirable peer groups to feel they are accepted.

9) often turn to alcohol and drugs to cope with the stresses of their life.

10) have been known to commit suicide.

11) have married too young as a means of getting away from unkind and selfish authority.

12) often become adults who abuse their families because unkindness is the only behavior they know.

13) have difficulty assuming the responsibilities of jobs, marriage and children when they become adults.

14) often need psychiatric help to relieve some of their emotional pain
and inability to cope with life.

15) often engage in stealing, vandalism,
violence and murder to get even
because they were hurt.

16) often become the people who fill the
jails. (Crime existed long before the
invention of television; however,
television violence can encourage
the acts of crime in those who have
been dealt with, as children, in an
unkind, selfish and blaming manner. Children who have been dealt
with in a loving manner are far less
apt to be influenced by television
violence.)

17) can become world leaders who
advocate wars to satisfy their emotional need for unkind power and
control just as their parents did in
disciplining them. Or, they may
become world leaders who know
only unkind power as a means of
solving problems.

As a result of unkind discipline children usually
become overaggressive, defiant, rebellious, hostile, have
a need to get even with unkind authority and are prone

fight, hit, kick, or bully others. Or, they may become submissive, compliant, obedient, depressed and with-drawn from others.

Dr. Thomas Gordon, in *Parent Effectiveness Training*, described children who have become submissive due to unkind discipline:

> Some children continue to be sub-missive and compliant through adoles-cence and often into adulthood. . . . These are the adults who remain chil-dren throughout their lives, passively submitting to authority, denying their own needs, fearing to be themselves, frightened of conflict, too compliant to stand up for their own convictions. These are adults who fill the offices of psychologists and psychiatrists.

I can verify Dr. Gordon's statement because he describes my personality during my teen and early adult years. As a child, I was obedient and depressed as the result of being spanked and whipped with a razor strap. My parents referred to me as their good little girl, not realizing that I was an emotionally sick child. As an adult I recognized my emotional problems. I overcame some of my emotional problems by studying psychology; how-ever, I have learned from personal experience that it is impossible to completely eradicate childhood emotional scars.

Children who are disciplined with unkindness can turn to God and *learn to use Biblical love* in their relationships; therefore, they can overcome some of the undesirable effects of having been unkindly treated in their childhood. *They can avoid following their parent's example of unkind discipline by learning to discipline in the kind way Jesus was disciplined,* and study books which support non-threatening discipline and give a good understanding of children's emotional development.

Excerpts Dealing With Spanking

Benjamin Spock and Michael B. Rothenberg, *Dr. Spock's Baby and Child Care*, 40th edition, (Pocket Books, New York: 1985), p. 408.

> There are several reasons to try to avoid physical punishment, I feel. It teaches children that the larger, stronger person has the power to get his way, whether or not he is in the right, and they may resent this in their parent— for life. Some spanked children feel quite justified in beating up on smaller ones. The American tradition of spanking may be one cause of the fact that there is much more violence in our country than in any other comparable nation—murder, armed robbery, wife abuse, child abuse.

Dorothy Corkille Briggs, *Your Child's Self-Esteem* (Doubleday, Garden City, New York: 1975), p. 234.

Every spanking fills a child with negative feelings that may be translated into further misbehavior. Whether the resulting anger is turned outward or inward, the fact remains that children have feelings about being spanked, and these feelings work against the best interest of parent and child.

Spanking does not teach inner conviction. It teaches fear, deviousness, lying, and aggression. No matter how we slice it, spanking is a physical assault of a bigger person on a smaller one. And yet we tell children they shouldn't hit someone smaller or weaker.

We can all smile at the apparent contradiction of the mother who slaps her child, saying, "I'll teach you not to hit!" Yet, studies show that youngsters subjected to overt parental aggression are far more likely to be physically aggressive and hostile in their relations with others.

The Willful and Dominating Personality

A dominating parent is usually inflexible, having the need to control his children at all times. The dominating and willful parent is determined to have his own way without concern for his child's needs (especially his emotional well being). Children follow the parents' example. In so doing, the child becomes a willful child determined to have his own way just as the parent does in dealing with him. In other words, a willful child has a willful parent. The battle is on. The willful parent can win by using unkind action, such as spanking, to over-power the younger child, but when the child becomes older, the parent loses his advantage of size and strength. Then the parent has little means to control his child. To give an example: As a means of control, a willful parent took the car keys from his young adult son. The son over-powered his parent simply by going to the neighbors to borrow their car.

The dominating personality:

1) Often has no concern for the emotional welfare of others. However, he usually does have concern for the physical needs of others.

2) Often knows love only for those who

supply his selfish needs—I need you to satisfy my need for sex, affection, romance, admiration and pleasure— I need you to support me financially—I need you to assume my responsibilities.

3) Often has a need to control others just as his parents controlled him.

4) Often is envious, possessive or jealous because he lacked security and love as a child.

5) Often is impulsive because, as a child, he was not allowed or taught to consider the pro's and con's of a situation before acting or speaking. He can also be impulsive because of hypersensitivity resulting from feeling unloved and insecure as a child. (Of course, hypersensitivity can be caused by a physical problem.)

6) Often is hypocritical. He can be loving when he wants to be.

7) Often is unkind and selfish with others (especially with his spouse and children; however, he always expects others to be kind and unselfish when dealing with him).

8) Often lies to defend his wrongdoing to avoid punishment or disapproval as he did during his childhood.

9) Often degrades others to build himself up because of low self-esteem, which resulted from experiences with his parents, such as being dominated and receiving "put-downs" or other unkind and selfish actions.

10) Often cannot hold jobs where he has to take instructions. He has to be the boss or work alone. He resents the instruction of others just as he resented his parent's dominating instructions.

11) Often does not see himself as the cause of a problem; therefore, he blames others for the problems he creates. For example: My father blamed me for being a nervous child not realizing it was his selfish and unkind actions which caused me to be a hyper and impulsive child.

12) Often resents advice, correction, and a difference of opinion.

Recommended Books for Further Study

It is strongly recommended that the following books be studied to gain a better insight and understanding of child behavior and emotional growth, as well as information for adults.

Bessell, Harold. *The Love Test*, New York: William Morrow & Co., 1984, helps us to understand the difference between romantic attraction and infatuation. It also explains the difference between emotional maturity and immaturity and how to build mature love.

Faber, Adele, and Elaine Mazlish. *How to Talk So Kids Will Listen and Listen So Kids Talk*, New York: Avon Books, 1982, will bring about more cooperation from children than all the yelling and pleading in the world.

Girdano, Daniel A. and George S. Everly, Jr. *Controlling Stress & Tension*, New Jersey: Prentice-Hall, 1979.

Gordon, Thomas. *Parent Effectiveness Training*, New York: David McKay Company, 1976, when thoroughly understood and executed does not support permissiveness. Dr. Gordon's theory of reasoning with children, rather than using unkind power to teach children right from wrong, supports Biblical love. Highly recommended.

Gordon, Thomas with Noel Burch. *Teacher Effectiveness Training*, New York: Peter H. Wyden, 1974.

Gordon, Thomas with Judith Gordon Sands. *P.E.T. in Action*, New York: Peter Wyden, 1976, explains some common misunderstanding of his theory.

McCoy, Kathleen. *Coping with Teenage Depression*, New York: NAL (New American Library), 1982.

National Committee for Prevention of Child Abuse. 332 S. Michigan Ave., Suite 1250, Chicago, IL 60604. Write for their N.C.P.C.A. Catalog. Many books are available on child raising in a kind manner.

Spock, Benjamin and Michael B. Rothenberg. *Dr. Spock's Baby and Child Care*, 40th edition, New York: Pocket Books, 1985.

Ulene, Art, and Steven Shelov. *Bringing Out the Best in Your Baby*, New York: Macmillan Publishing, 1986, explains the physical and emotional development of children from birth to age four.